Desert Animals

by Lydia Carlin

SCHOLASTIC INC.

NEW YORK • TORONTO • LONDON • AUCKLAND • SYDNEY • MEXICO CITY • NEW DELHI • HONG KONG

Photographs © 2011: age fotostock/Juniors Bildarchiv: 5; Alamy Images/Picture Press: 3; iStockphoto: 8 (Bartosz Hadyniak), 1 (Eric Isselée), 6 (Bruno Buongiorno Nardelli); Media Bakery: 2; Photo Researchers, NY: 7 (Steve Cooper), 4 (Francesco Tomasinelli); ShutterStock, Inc./mlorenz: cover.

ISBN 978-0-545-34808-9

Cover and interior design by Holly Grundon. Photo research by Veroniqua Quinteros.

Copyright © 2011 by Lefty's Editorial Services. All rights reserved. Published by Scholastic Inc.
SCHOLASTIC, GUIDED SCIENCE READERS, and associated logos are trademarks and/or registered trademarks of Scholastic Inc.

16 15 14 13 12   17 18 19 20 21/0

Printed in the U.S.A.   08

First printing, September 2011

Let's meet some desert animals.

Let's meet a kangaroo.
It can leap.

Let's meet a spider.
It can creep.

Let's meet a fox.
It can sleep.

Let's meet a lizard.
It can hide.

Let's meet a snake.
It can slide.

Let's meet a camel.
It can take you for a ride!